HEAVEN'S OIL

ENEMIES OF THE ANOINTING

MARILYN REED

Copyright © 2011
Heaven's Oil: Enemies of the Anointing
Marilyn Reed
P.O. Box 6422
Pine Bluff, AR. 71611
E-mail: maguy.reed@hotmail.com

Printed in the United States of America

Library of Congress – Catalogued in Publication Data

ISBN 978-0-9839248-6-9

All rights reserved. No part of this book may be reproduced, stored in a retrieval system, or transmitted in any form or by any means, electronic, mechanical photocopying, recording, or otherwise, without written consent of the publisher except in the case of brief quotations in critical articles or reviews.

Unless otherwise indicated, all Scripture quotations are taken from the King James Version of the Bible.

Editorial Assistance
Jabez Books Writers' Agency
A Division of Clark's Consultant Group
www.clarksconsultantgroup.com

Acknowledgments

First and foremost, I would like to give God the glory and thank Him for being my Abba Father. I bow my knee to you. To my Lord and Savior Jesus Christ, I'm eternally grateful. I'm honored to have been a co-writer with the Holy Spirit in writing this bestseller book on behalf of the Kingdom of God.

And to my husband, U. S. Reed, I thank you for being there for me. It was challenging enough to write while in trial after trial; yet, you encouraged me to keep writing. Thanks for your patience and know that I love you always.

To God be the glory for my children. To my son Alex, you are my quiet storm, thank you for having a listening ear. I would like to thank my beautiful daughter Toni who has learned how to "trust God!" To my grandchildren, McKenzie and Adyson, because of the two of you, life is sweeeeeeet!

Next, I would like to give a hug and much thanks to Jan Whitaker for inviting me to her book writing seminar. For your support, I am eternally grateful. Maryland Johnson thanks for your friendship and for your earnest and effectual prayers.

And finally, I thank you Dr. Shirley K. Clark, my consultant and Clark Consultant Group for the role they played in making this book a reality. Thank you for sharing with me and believing in me. The many hours you spent to make this book a bestseller, I will without end be grateful!

Dedication

This book is dedicated to my friend, Holy Spirit and all who have a respect for heaven's oil (the anointing).

TABLE OF CONTENTS

INTRODUCTION

CHAPTER ONE:	The Anointing	11
CHAPTER TWO:	Forsaking Prayer	31
CHAPTER THREE:	Pride	48
CHAPTER FOUR:	Cold Love	66
CHAPTER FIVE:	Grieving the Holy Spirit	85
CHAPTER SIX:	A Religious Spirit	101

Introduction

This book is a result of my learning to value the anointing of God that is within me and upon my life. This book was birthed out of a longing in me to operate in the anointing of God and experience results. From my own experience, I know what it is like to preach and not have the anointing of God present to be effective. What a disheartening and intimidating feeling. I learned quickly that the anointing of God is never to be taken for granted. I began to examine myself to see if there was anything going on in my life that was contrary to the will of God. I didn't want anything in my life that would be a barrier to me receiving a greater anointing from God. Whatever the hindrance was, without any condemnation I simply said,

"Holy Spirit here am I, train me in the things of the Lord."

The purpose of this book is to arouse and stir up the people of God to hunger and thirst for a greater anointing that will equip them to live a life of triumph. I pray that after reading this book you will desire God to use you as a laborer in the vineyard to destroy the works of the enemy. In this book I touched on just a few subjects that I call "enemies of the anointing" that I felt were hindrances to receiving a greater anointing. As you read this book, keep in mind that a lifestyle of sin will stop the flow of Heaven's Oil in your life, and hinder you from being able to do the works of Christ and be effective. It is essential to have "Heaven's Oil" (the anointing) to function in the power and glory as the disciples of Christ did in times past. That same power is available to us today. So whatever it takes, lay aside every weight (sin) that would stop the flow of that power from operating and flowing through you! Remember, in a great house there are vessels of honor and some of dishonor; therefore, let the Holy Spirit purge you to be sanctified vessels; meet for the Master's use.

Chapter One

The Anointing

The anointing can be defined in a myriad of ways. The one that is pertinent to this book is that it is supernatural or heavenly enablement. It is the manifested power and presence of the Holy Spirit operating in the life of a person to bring to pass the works of Jesus Christ. It is the power and presence of the Holy Spirit enabling a person to perform a task or function in an office he or she is called and appointed to do. As believers, we should greatly desire to have the anointing of God flowing in our lives. If we want to be prepared to effectively do the will of the Father, as our Messiah did and be victorious in doing even greater works; we must be anointed.

In the Old Testament, God gave Moses instructions on how to prepare special oil that was called "the oil of the anointing." This anointing oil was to be used for the service of God within the Tabernacle. The Priest, along with the furnishings in the Tabernacle were expected to be anointed. Also in the Old Testament, there were two other kind of leaders that were to be anointed for their ministries: (a) Kings (1 Samuel 10: 1) and (b) Prophets (1 Kings 19:16).

Moreover, the Lord spake unto Moses, saying Take thou also unto thee principal spices, of pure myrrh five hundred shekels, and of sweet cinnamon half so much, even two hundred and fifty shekels, and of sweet calamus two hundred and fifty shekels, and of cassia five hundred shekels after the shekel of the sanctuary, and of olive oil an hin: and thou shalt make it an oil of holy ointment, an ointment compound after the art of the apothecary: it shall be an holy anointing oil.

Exodus 30: 22-25

In the Old Testament, the ingredients for the anointing oil are symbolic of what God requires from believers so that the anointing can flow freely. As we look at the importance of each ingredient or spice, we will understand the attributes or character of a person anointed with this oil.

Elements of the Anointing Oil

The oil of the anointing was to be composed of specific elements that were to be ground up in order to produce the final product.

1. **Myrrh:** The word myrrh comes from the Hebrew murr or maror, which means bitter. Myrrh was the first spice mentioned by God in the composition of the oil. In the Bible myrrh is always associated with bitterness and suffering. For example, when Naomi had experienced the loss of her husband and two sons in the country of Moab; she no longer wanted to be called Naomi, but Mara, because of her bitter experience (see Ruth 1). Myrrh is very bitter in taste, and not at all appealing to the appetite.

Although bitter, it produces a fragrance that's somewhat pleasing; therefore, it had great value in biblical times. During the times of Jesus, it was used as incense burned during funerals until the 15th century. History tells us that the Roman Emperor Nero burned a year's supply of myrrh at the funeral of his wife Poppea Sabina in the year 65 C.E. When considering the ingredient myrrh, know that there will be circumstances and situations of bitterness that believers in Christ will experience that are essential in the development of Christ like character. As hard as it may be, you are to value the bitter experiences, for they are only preparing you for the anointing. When life gets hard for a believer, it helps to understand that the loads we carry are a refining process. That refining process will help eliminate enemies of the anointing such as pride, cold love, envy, self-will, jealousy, just to name a few. In your search for "Heaven's Oil", you will find that most of your experiences will be bitter rather than sweet. Myrrh was also used in biblical times to anoint a body prior to burial; therefore myrrh also speaks to us of death to "self" in the life of the believer. Remember, God does not anoint flesh (carnality). Upon man's flesh, it shall not be poured (see Exodus 30: 32). Remember, God's instructions to Moses concerning myrrh (the bitter); it was to be **twice** that of sweet cinnamon and sweet calamus. Isn't that interesting, we must first partake of the bitter before we share in the sweetness, which leads me to the next ingredient of the oil.

2. **Sweet Cinnamon**: The second ingredient used in the making of the oil is sweet cinnamon. It comes from the bark of a tree and has a certain fragrant sweetness. One of the meanings of the word cinnamon in the Hebrew is "erect" (upright). It means to erect or stand upright. As carriers of God's anointing we must walk in integrity and truth before God and man. We are living in a time where God's people are challenged to divinely influence a lost and

corrupt society; without it influencing and perverting them. The Word of God teaches believers that we are the salt of the earth, but if the salt has lost his savour, (strength, and its ability to influence) wherewith shall it be salted (see Matthew 5:13a). It is going to take the anointing of God to influence a heart cloaked in darkness. If you desire for Heaven's Oil to be smeared upon your life, you can't be bound and yoked up with sin. You must be like the cinnamon erect "upright" before God and man. We live in a world where sin is all around us, and although sin may stink with a foul odor so to speak; we must remain sweet in the anointing. We will often have to encounter and confront disagreeable and unpleasant situations in life, but if you will yield to the sweet anointing of the Holy Spirit to rule in the midst of that situation, it will be well with you. No matter what comes your way, you are to be like cinnamon "upright" and not bow down to enemies or to circumstances, but remain "sweet," at peace, allowing others to smell (discern) the sweet aroma of God that governs your life. **For we are unto God a sweet savour of Christ, in them that are saved, and in them that perish (2 Corinthians 2:15).**

3. **Sweet Calamus**: This was the third ingredient in the oil of the anointing. Calamus in Hebrew is the word "qaneh" meaning a reed. This type of reed could be used as a measuring rod which could grow and reach about ten feet in height. **And there was given to me a reed like unto a rod: and the angel stood, saying rise, and measure the temple of God, and the altar, and them that worship therein (Revelation 11:1).**

   The worshippers will be measured as to whether they make God's glory their ultimate, and His word their final authority in all their acts of worship. We will be measured in the house of God to know whether our worship is in a hypocritical, false and counterfeit manner with insincere hearts. God will measure to see if the church has trodden under foot his grace;

leading lifestyles that are not pleasing to Him; thereby, frustrating the grace of God. The Lord will also measure our level of intimacy with Him. We do not want to be counted among those who have done many things in His name but never **knew** him (see Matthew 7:21-23). One connotation for the word knew in Hebrew is the word intimate. The Bible says that Adam knew his wife and she conceived and bore him a son. We must spend time with the Lord to get to know him in an intimate way. When we know him in such a way; we will begin to understand His will and our destiny will be conceived and birthed. If we desire Heaven's Oil to flow freely in our lives, we must spend time with the Lord. Always remember, God can entrust His anointing to an individual that spends time with Him, communes with Him and loves on Him.

Sweet calamus was a tall reed that grew in a hostile environment, which was swampy and muddy somewhat like miry clay. It always stands erect even in muddy waters. Calamus speaks to us to live and abide in Christ come what may. We are to stand tall in Him knowing whatever the issues of life are; all is well because of the Lord. The anointing requires us to abide in Him and commune with Him. In this life you will have experiences that seem as though you are under hostile attack on every hand. You may even at times have experiences that make you feel as though the valley you are in is impassable. Calamity and trouble can seem as though you're swimming in a lake of misery; but you stand. The anointing of God helps us to stand and be strong, especially if you are experiencing a miry pit. Don't ever lie down in the pit, like the calamus stand tall in the Lord and in the power of His might.

4. **Cassia**: The fourth component in the "oil of the anointing" is found in the bark of a shrub like the ingredient cinnamon. The word cassia in the Hebrew carries with it the mindset of bowing and humbling. The root word actually

means to bow down as in bowing before God in reverence of Him. Cassia speaks of humility, which should be the attitude or characteristic of a person who is flowing in the anointing of God. The anointing should not make us self-possessed (having a firm belief in one's own powers), but quite the opposite. Anointed or not, we are to humble ourselves before a mighty God. Peter admonishes us to humble yourselves therefore under the mighty hand of God, that He may exalt you in due time (1 Peter 5: 16). If there be no humility, you face falling into the cesspool of pride. This will cause the flow of the anointing to cease and a person will end up being humiliated trying to do the works of Christ in their own powers. Remember, the seven sons of Sceva, a Jewish priest at Ephesus (see Acts 19:13-16). The seven sons of Sceva, perhaps motivated by pride, walked into a battle unprepared. They tried to cast out an unclean spirit from a man and were unsuccessful. The possessed man leaps on them and overpowers them. The seven sons run away naked, wounded and humiliated. This whole episode should caution us in wielding the name of Jesus without a real relationship with Him. Always remember, a greater anointing is just one way God promotes His vessels, so stay humble.

5. **Olive Oil:** The final ingredient in the "oil of the anointing" is the olive oil. This is the ingredient that binds and holds together all the spices. This is a picture of the sweet and bitter coming together. Men and women of God that are carriers of His anointing will not have a choice just to accept life circumstances that are sweet; but the bitter has to be experienced also.

This element of the oil is the product of the olive tree. The olive tree was one of the main tree crops of Israel. The word olive draws its meaning from the word illumination, thereby producing illuminating oils. Some studies show that it can take up to two to three years for an olive tree to mature, and then the fruit ripens slowly. The olive tree is able to survive long periods of drought. The olive oil speaks to us in being able to survive the drought and dry seasons in life, when it seems as though life's circumstances are not in your favor. The fact that it could take a few years before the fruit of the olive tree matures should convey a message to us that as carriers of God's anointing; we should be mature in the Lord. Sometimes the maturing process in the life of a believer takes years. God does not anoint a novice. Would you give the keys to your car to a six year old? Character has to be tried and tested, and afterwards, you will come forth in due season -- illuminated, producing fruit, conditioned and enabled to do the works of Jesus. Like the olive tree, when experiencing a drought, stay encouraged knowing that there is a process that you must endure in order for the olive (the anointing) to come forth in your life. A person made ready for the anointing is a person that has gone through a process of brokenness and death (dying to self). It is sometimes in your dry season that the Lord wants some things in your character to die. In dying to self, know that a loving God awaits a dying you; when you can truly say "it's no longer my will, but Yours." Allow the life of Jesus to be your greatest example in yielding to the will of God. Submit to the Lord and yield to the Holy Spirit, who knows how to shape, form and fashion a vessel fit for the Master's use. There will be no short cuts and neither are there any gimmicks in flowing in the anointing; it's only through the grace of the Holy Spirit. So we see that there were five elements blended together to make up the holy anointing oil. The number five is significant in that it represents the grace of God. It is only because of God's abundant grace that we are able to experience the anointing of the Holy Spirit.

In the Old Testament, the oil of the anointing would be poured upon three groups of leaders in preparation for their ministries: Kings, Priests and

Prophets. Today we receive the anointing by the grace of the Holy Spirit. However, there is still a process that a person will go through in order to be approved by God to walk in a heavy anointing or a high level of the anointing. Yes, you will be tested or tried by God. The word tried or tested in Greek is the word "dokimos." It simply means approval. On the underside of many ancient pieces of pottery, you would find the word "dokimos". If the piece of pottery had gone through the furnace and wasn't cracked; it would be marked "dokimos", and would be approved for use. God's chosen vessels that have been tried in the furnace and approved for His service are spiritually marked "dokimos". There is a trial and a testing by God that will reveal the deepest intentions of an individual's heart. God will anoint those for His service that walk in integrity, who refuse to depreciate their position for God and the things of God into a false, counterfeit, pseudo performance. In your time in the furnace, you may lose some friends, at times feel lonely, rejected and **extremely misunderstood**; cry if you will; but bear in mind, you are being approved by God. Remember, when being approved and anointed by God, you don't have to become desperate or anxious for ministry. Take heed because desperation will allow for others to shape you into becoming something less than what the Lord God Almighty planned and purposed for you to be. Selah!

In order for the Body of Christ to be effective in destroying the works of the enemy and for deliverance to take place, we need the power and anointing of God. Whatever the yoke of Satan may be, the anointing of God will destroy it. Without the anointing, a person will simply be operating in the flesh, and no good thing will come from the exercise of your flesh. It profits nothing.

Before I move into the enemies of the anointing, let's look at the empowerment and purpose of the anointing upon the life of Jesus. On the Sabbath, Jesus stood in the synagogue and read aloud from the scroll of Isaiah a passage of scripture declaring the purpose of the anointing.

THE SPIRIT OF THE *LORD IS UPON ME*, BECAUSE HE HATH ANOINTED ME TO PREACH THE GOSPEL TO THE POOR; HE HATH SENT ME TO HEAL THE BROKENHEARTED, TO PREACH

DELIVERANCE TO THE CAPTIVES, AND RECOVERY OF SIGHT TO THE BLIND, TO SET AT LIBERTY THEM THAT ARE BRUISED, TO PREACH THE ACCEPTABLE YEAR OF THE LORD.

Luke 4:18-19

The purpose of the anointing is to glorify the Father; the *Mantle of Power* will not rest upon glory-seekers. In this passage of scripture we will see six purposes of the anointing.

1. Empowers you to preach: The good news we proclaim about Jesus and the Kingdom of God; the anointing enables you to be effective in doing so. Anointed preaching penetrates the veil of flesh and reaches into the spirit and soul of man, bringing forth deliverance, illumination, healing, revelation, transformation and a renewed mind.

2. To heal the brokenhearted: Brokenhearted here means to crush completely, complete ruin, destruction, to break in pieces. These would be the hard cases you will encounter as you proclaim the gospel -- "good news". As you minister under the anointing, you will be able to console those who are deeply afflicted or whose hearts are broken by external trials, struggles and calamity. Only Heaven's Oil (the anointing) will enable you to impact the brokenhearted reassuring them that Jesus has a balm of consolation for the brokenhearted.

3. To preach deliverance to the captives: If you are a carrier of God's anointing, you are somebody's Moses; somebody's "deliverer," even if it's just one person. Moses delivered a nation (multitude) out of Egypt. We have heard it taught that Egypt represents the world; we are anointed to preach deliverance to those being held captive by the world. God has empowered

us to reach those who have sighed long in captivity. When a person is in captivity and has a sighing in their spirit; that means they are taking in and letting out a deep audible breath for relief from weariness. Anointed preaching will bring deliverance to those that sin has enslaved, mastered and are sighing in their spirits -- to be set free from spiritual darkness. The anointing of God will minister to and destroy any yoke that holds the mind of a person in captivity. Satan has raped (violated) the minds of so many people, cloaking them in darkness from receiving Jesus as their Lord and Savior. He has sold them a "bill of goods" to believe that they are not good enough or they have to stop sinning before they come to Christ. These lies, along with a multitude of others spoken to the mind of many by Satan the "father of lies," have held the captive in captivity too long.

4. Recovery of sight to the blind: The blind are those who in every way are miserable and destitute of all hope of salvation. You are anointed to minister -- "you are the light of the world." You are anointed to share Jesus to them that sit in darkness. To them that need eye salve; Jesus has it, and it is ours for the asking. We are anointed by the power of His grace to guide the blind or unregenerate soul to the "Light of the World" -- Jesus Christ our Lord and Savior.

5. To set at liberty them that are bruised: The word bruised here refers to those who are pressed down by tragedy, calamity and hurts. Many are the bruised that have suffered emotionally, but keep that hurt hid under a thin skin of "I'm ok"; ashamed to say "I need help". These are they that have a need to be freed from this pressure and rest in the grace and consolation of the Lord. The Jesus in you will be able to reach the bruised and bring comfort to a heart

that has housed anxiety, heaviness, and stress and strain.

6. To preach the Acceptable Year of the Lord: This alludes to the Year of Jubilee when both the debtors and servants were set free. Jesus Christ is our Jubilee and who the Son sets free is free indeed. Christ is our kinsman redeemer, a Savior that has set us free from having to be a slave to sin.

Before leaving this earth realm, Jesus spoke to His disciples saying that whoever trusts in me will also do the works I do and even greater works. The works continued on through the Apostles and may they continue through you till the return of the Lord. May the Spirit of the Living God work through you; giving spiritual life to the spiritually dead. You are somebody's Moses, a man by the hand of God who helped deliver a nation. Who will you help deliver, by sharing Jesus?

Chapter Two

Forsaking Prayer

Prayer is a privilege and it is a key to operating in the anointing. Men and women of God who have done great exploits knew their God. They spent time with God in private prayer; seeking the face of God and becoming intimate with Him. It is in your prayer time that you will discover your total dependency upon God for spiritual strength. If you desire to operate in a greater level of the anointing; not for some egotistical, self-seeking reason, but for the glory of God to be manifested; you must be steadfast in prayer.

I can recall moments in my life when before regular church service would start prayer was to go forth in the sanctuary, but very few people would show up for prayer. This would always amaze me, well to be honest, it would annoy me knowing how important prayer is; yet people just didn't come to prayer for whatever the reason. In those moments I remember saying prayer sets the atmosphere for the anointing of God to descend. Prayer will set the atmosphere for miracles to take place. Prayer is much needed to invite and welcome the Holy Spirit. I would cry out, "Why won't people come out for prayer?" Well needless to say, to those who know the importance of prayer; when you find yourself in corporate prayer and the only people who show up is you and the sound man; pray like there's no tomorrow! Jesus delivered us from being concerned about numbers when He stated where two or three are gathered together in my name, there am I in the midst of them (Matt.18:20.) You see, the Jews believed in what is called a minyan. A minyan was a group of 10 adult Jews required for a valid meeting and the most common activity requiring a minyan was public prayer. Jesus was saying that the tradition of men requires 10 to pray, but I will be in the midst of two or three. God honors our faithfulness to prayer. God is not impressed with numbers, but he will honor those who commune with Him. One of the honors He bestows upon a praying person is the anointing. God will not entrust His anointing to individuals who do not pray.

As Christians, we are called to a lifestyle of prayer. Every Christian has a responsibility to pray. **Pray without ceasing (1 Thessalonians 5:17).**

I exhort therefore, that first of all, supplication, prayers, intercessions and giving of thanks be made for all men.
1 Timothy 2:1

Our Messiah, the Lord Jesus Christ was a man of prayer. "Christ" in the Greek means "the Anointing." If Jesus Christ, the Anointed One lived a life of prayer, shouldn't we do the same? Jesus set aside His glory and took on the mantle of flesh (Philippians 2:5-8), and while on earth, He was obedient to the Father; and He prayed! He had a prayer life because of His dependence upon the Father. Jesus said, "I can of mine own self do nothing; as I hear, I judge; and My judgment is just; because I seek not mine own will, but the will of the Father which hath sent me (John 5:30)". No one will be effective in doing the will of God without the anointing and a strong prayer life. Just because God has called and chosen you, does not mean you do not have to pray. Because prayer was such a priority in the life of Jesus, He would find Himself praying all night.

And it came to pass in those days that he went out into a mountain to pray, and continued all night in prayer to God.
Luke 6:12

Prior to this all night prayer meeting with God, Jesus had come under attack by the scribes and Pharisees (religious folk), for healing a man on the Sabbath. Then after being in prayer all night, Jesus chose His twelve disciples. Intimacy with God is an investment; it cultivates our relationship with Him. It is in those intimate moments that Heaven's Oil (the anointing) is smeared upon your life. Jesus had to deal with His enemies and at the same time; He had to make decisions concerning His ministry. As Christians, when we spend time with the Lord, all night if need be, time invested in prayer and fellowship will result in you knowing how to deal with your enemies and how to know the will of God for your life. We are invited to sit down and have a one on one conversation with the **One** who knows all things. Our ministry to God is far more important than our ministry to men. Our time alone with God, will allow the anointing to flow; thereby, having an overflow to minister to others. And that's what it's all about being empowered to be effective in sharing Jesus to a hurting world.

In Luke 5:16, the scripture says that Jesus withdrew himself into the wilderness and prayed. Again, Jesus made spending time alone with God a priority. Luke 5:17 gives us great insight into how the overflow of the anointing is for others. This passage of scripture tells us that on a certain day Jesus was teaching, and there were Pharisees and doctors of the law sitting by, which had come out of every town of Galilee, Judea and Jerusalem; and the power of God was present to heal them. The Bible goes on to say that a man was healed of palsy. So we see Jesus, in these passages of scripture going from praying to ministering to those that needed healing. The power of the Lord was present to heal them because Jesus had spent intimate time with the Father; ministered to Him first and then unto mankind. The way we minister to people is by allowing the overflow of the anointing and power that we have received in our time alone with the Lord; to pour out and be shared with others. Remember, much prayer, much power! Again, as I mentioned earlier, God will not entrust Heaven's Oil to individuals who won't spend time with Him. We are co-laborers with the Lord. I'm reminded of a quote by St. Augustine: **"Without God we cannot; without us God will not."**

Moshe Rabbenu (Moses), the lawgiver, prophet and God's chosen leader was a co-laborer with God in getting the children of Israel out of Egypt. Moses was a praying man; a man that God spoke to face-to-face. The word for face-to-face in Hebrew is the word "al-peney." This is pronounced al-pin-ay. It means to be face to face and in the presence of. This word also means to turn oneself, to turn towards and to face, to be in front or forepart. Moses had an "al-peney" relationship with the Holy One of Israel.

> **And the LORD spake unto Moses face to face, as a man speaketh unto his friend.**
> **Exodus 33:11**

Moses' divine mission in the earth was made known to him as he communed with God. Moses was a man that was conscious of his human limitations which drove him to seek God in prayer. Moses' life should be an example to us. No matter what your limitations are, God will equip you to do what He has called you to do. He was a hero to the Hebrew people; yet, human like us. He knew in order to walk in the plan, purpose and the will of God; he must have communion with God to take counsel from the Holy One of Israel. As we concentrate on Moses' heroic exploits; never forget his secret weapon was a face-to-face relationship with God. I believe prayer was a part of his everyday life like eating and sleeping. Thank God for Moses, the **"Deliverer"** of Israel and thank God for you; because you are somebody's deliverer. It might be a co-worker, the prostitute on the streets, the drug addict, someone being abused by a spouse or the stranger in the grocery store; deliverance is much needed in these last and evil days. Whomever or whatever the case may be; ask the Lord to endow you with His anointing and order your steps so that when your paths cross someone who is in Egypt (the world); the power of God will rest upon you to "set the captive free." In a dark and evil world, there's a multitude that's waiting for someone to deliver them out of Egypt; to snatch them out of the clutches of Satan. You are somebody's Moses. Having the anointing of the Holy Spirit, the power of God within you; go forth and confuse and confound the kingdom of darkness. Someone once said, "God is not looking for great ability; He's just looking for availability." I admonish you to avail yourselves unto Him in prayer and watch God anoint you to walk in your divine mission in the earth.

We must never forget that the purpose of the anointing is not to make us famous with the masses; but to minister the power and the life of Jesus to others. In the history of Moses, we see that the congregation of

Israel was disgruntled and murmured against Moses. He was a liberator; yet, he at times was not popular with the people, and so it will be with you, God's anointed. Your adversary, the devil persecutes the anointing because Satan knows God's anointed servants can destroy the yoke of the enemy and ruin his plans of death and defeat in a person's life. Think it not strange if you are a carrier of God's anointing and you come under the attack of the enemy. Think it not strange the people the devil will use to attack you; sometimes it's your family, friends, co-workers and even church folk.

> **The kings of the earth set themselves, and the rulers take counsel together against the Lord and against his anointed.**
> **Psalm 2:2**

Be not dismayed at the persecution you shall encounter because of Heaven's Oil upon your life. Endure the persecution and continue to seek the Lord with a whole heart so that you will truly know how to count it all joy!

Another example of one of the heroes in the Bible that was a man of prayer was Elijah. He was an ordinary man used by God because he was a man of effectual fervent prayer. The book of James tells us this about Elijah.

Elijah was a man subject to like passions as we are, and he prayed earnestly that it might not rain, and it rained not on the earth by the space of three years and six months. And he prayed again and the heaven gave rain, and the earth brought forth her fruit.
James 5:17-18

The great prophet Elijah lived during the dark days of Israel's apostasy. This was a time in history when Ahab and Jezebel ruled the land and had turned it over to the worship of the pagan god Baal; a pagan god of nature and fertility. Elijah's name means "Jehovah is God." What a befitting name for a prophet of the true God in a nation and time given over to idol worship. Elijah's divine mission in the earth was to turn the nation of Israel back to Yahweh, the Almighty God of Israel. Here we have Elijah; a man clothed in humanity, "a man of like passions as we," yet knew he would prevail by faith and being devoted to prayer. Instead of succumbing and surrendering to idolatry and the political structure of that day, Elijah sought refuge in the LORD through prayer. He knew in order to face the challenges set before him; he had to get alone with God. What a great privilege and benefit we have through prayer to get alone with the LORD. Can you think of any greater honor than to have a one-on-one audience with the ONE who rules over all creation? I encourage you not to let such a privilege as this lay dormant. I admonish you not to let the devil silence your voice especially where prayer is concerned. It is evident that a life of prayer speaks volumes of a person's dependency upon God. We cannot survive without prayer. Sure you can exist but there's a vast difference in surviving and existing; our survival depends upon faith, grace and much prayer.

Jehovah is God is the meaning of the prophet Elijah's name. Let's look at some of his victories in the name of Jehovah.

- He revived the son of the widow of Zarephat (1 Kings 17:22)

- He defended the worship of Jehovah God (1 Kings 18:21)
- He defeated the priest of Baal (1 Kings 18)
- He prophesied with power and precision (1 Kings17:1)
- He called down fire from heaven (2 Kings 1:9-12)

These are just a few of many great feats of Elijah. The great exploits done by this heroic prophet, speaks volumes of the confidence that he had in his relationship with the Holy One of Israel -- "blessed be he." It was a relationship that was nurtured through prayer. If you are seeking the LORD for a greater anointing, never neglect so great a privilege as prayer. Through disciplined prayer you will become a "sharp-shooter" in the spirit realm. Meaning your prayers won't be all over the place; you'll know how to aim and target your prayers as you understand spiritual reality; a realm beyond our physical senses.

In the arena of spiritual reality, I'm reminded of Elisha, who was a man of prayer also, and the attendant and talmidim (disciple) of Elijah. Elisha understood spiritual reality as he asked God to open his servant's eyes so that they could see the chariots of protection in the spirit realm.

> **And he answered, fear not for they that be with us are more than they that be with them. And Elisha prayed, and said, LORD, I pray thee, open his eyes, that he may see. And the LORD opened the eyes of the young man; and he saw and behold the mountain was full of horses and chariots of fire round about Elisha.**
> **2 Kings 6:16-17**

We are no different than the saints of old. There are no substitutes or shortcuts to flowing in the power and anointing of God. Pray without ceasing was the way or method used by Moses, Elijah, Elisha, Jesus and His apostles. I cannot stress the importance of prayer in the life of the believer. There's a host of reasons why people don't pray. Some excuses are:

- There's not enough time
- Not disciplined enough

- Prayer is boring
- My mind wanders too much in prayer
- God already know my needs
- Guilt that drives an individual away from God
- Not experiencing immediate manifestation to prayer

Whatever the reason may be that's robbing you or someone you know out of their prayer life; be determined to press beyond your barriers to prayer and know that a loving Father awaits you. Daily communion with our Heavenly Father must be a priority in our lives. What a shame, we have time for everything else in life; but no time for fellowship with our Maker, our Savior and the Holy Spirit. Have we like Israel, gone whoring after other gods (Judges 2:17)? God is a jealous God. Who or what is sitting on the throne of your heart, besides El Shaddai- God Almighty? I dare not walk in condemnation because that's the devils job to condemn, but I am convicted when I know I have given too much of my time to frivolous and very unfruitful things. People can sit and watch a one hour movie, and play games on the computer for long periods of time; but only want to pray **(fellowship)** with God for ten minutes. Have I just described you? If so, there's no condemnation just repent and find your way into the Father's bosom, bask in His presence and love on Him for long as you like. He loves you and He welcomes your presence. I mentioned giving the Lord ten minutes of your time. I dare not put a time frame on the time you spend with the Lord. I think that's personal, but I do know that the more time you spend with Him; the more of Him you desire **over** T.V., long and sometimes empty phone conversations, hours on the computer and whatever else consumes the bulk of your time.

I believe one of the simplest prayers an individual can pray is "Hineni." The Hebrew meaning of this word is "Here Am I." When God called Abraham's name in Genesis 22:1, concerning the (Akeda) the offering up of Isaac, Abraham answered God, "Here Am I." When we read in 1 Samuel 3:1-4, we have a young Samuel asleep in the Temple at Shiloh, when God calls Samuel's name, he, thinking that it was the priest Eli, he answered "hineni" (Here am I). Another example of "hineni" can be found in Exodus 3:4; when God called unto Moses out of the midst of the burning bush, we see Moses answering God, "Here Am I."

If you find yourself struggling in prayer, needing to break through all kinds of barriers to prayer; just relax and tell the Father, "Hineni." LORD, "here am I. Here am I; ready to get to know You and have an intimate relationship with You. Here am I LORD, maybe not knowing Your will for my life; but nevertheless here am I. As you stand before a loving Father, your life may be in a state of confusion; just tell Him, here am I.

Here am I (hineni) is also a term for the most part used to convey readiness. Our heavenly Father awaits a people ready to do His will. And those that are excited about doing His will, He will anoint to be effective servants in the courts of the Lord and in the highways and byways of life. As you read this book, I can only hope that you will have a burning desire for the Lord to prepare your life to carry a heavy anointing. There's absolutely a price to pay; yet, worth it, because as you're reading this book; there's a harvest of souls being held captive by the yoke of the devil! I entreat you to sacrifice for others; become a prayer warrior, anointed with the power of the Holy Spirit to set the captive free.

Praying always with all prayer and supplication in the Spirit, and watching thereunto with all perseverance and supplication for all saints.

Ephesians 6:18

Chapter Three

Pride

Upon man's flesh shall it not be poured.
Exodus 30:32a

God gave instructions to Moses concerning the composition of the anointing oil and He told Moses that the anointing oil was not to be poured upon man's flesh. The anointing oil was precious, sanctified and set apart for a stated purpose. It was not to be taken as common oil; therefore, it was not to be rubbed on man's flesh. The anointing of God is everything but common and those individuals that are carriers of His anointing will tell you that the weight of

God's (kabod) glory upon their lives cost them dearly. Number one, self has to die; which leads me to the subject of pride, an enemy of the anointing. Pride has been defined in many ways. Pride is:

- A high sense of one's status or ego
- Proud or disdainful behavior or treatment
- The love of one's own excellence
- Having a high opinion of oneself
- Vanity and vainglory (self-idolatry)
- Feeling of superiority
- The quality of being arrogant
- A haughty outlook or attitude shown by somebody who believes "**often unjustifiably**" that he or she is superior to others

If there is any above definition you can identify with, just remember the attitude of pride acts as a barrier against receiving the grace of God. Pride is an enemy of the anointing. If you have never walked in pride or the sin of pride has never affected you, then I say unto you, "how great thou art." Pride can be so subtle and it can hide itself in the host or carrier to a degree that the person in pride won't even recognize the pride in them. There might not be the outward manifestation of bragging or looking down on others, but what about the sin of pride when we go ahead of God? Is it pride that tells us that after much supplication and tears, God is not moving so go ahead and do things our way? Pride can rear its ugly head in many ways; and because God has placed it at the very top of the list of things He hates (Proverbs 6:16-17a), no man is exempt from the spirit of pride making a knock at the door of their heart, so let's all be on guard against it.

    The manifestation of the anointing is one of the ways God exalts us. Humility is the opposite of pride and those that are promoted by God must clothe themselves in a spirit of humility or God will resist them. If you are seeking the Lord for a greater anointing to be effective in destroying the works of the enemy, pride will not be a part of your journey. James, the brother of our Messiah, counseled us when he warned, God resisteth the proud, but giveth grace unto the humble (James 4:6). The Apostle Peter exhorts us to humble ourselves; therefore, under the mighty hand of God, that He may exalt us in due time (1 Peter 5:6). We should always be aware that with humility comes exaltation or promotion and out of the bowels of pride will be birthed destruction, humiliation and possibly public condemnation.

As we examine pride in the Word of God, who better to start with than Lucifer and his (naphal) fall. In reading Isaiah 14:12-15, we see that it was self-exaltation (pride) that caused Lucifer to be cast down from heaven.

How art thou fallen from heaven, O Lucifer, son of the morning! How art thou cut down to the ground, which didst weaken the nations! For thou hast said in thine heart, I will ascend into heaven, I will exalt my throne above the stars of God: I will sit also upon the mount of the congregation, in the sides of the north: I will ascend above the heights of the clouds; I will be like the Most High.

Isaiah 14:12-15

Throughout history, pride has been Satan's identity. He knows that pride caused his fall; therefore, he uses pride in the life of a believer to bring forth their downfall. Satan's desire is for man to believe he can be self-sufficient (pride) and disconnected from God (pride). In Satan's downfall he used the language I call the "I syndrome." I will ascend, I will sit, I will ascend above, and I will be. Lucifer tapped into a form of self-idolatry, the worship of self and the need or desire to be worshiped. Lucifer (Satan) was already in an exalted position, yet pride wanted him to self-exalt himself. He was the anointed cherub that covereth (Ezekiel 28:14b). He was a picture of the highest of God's creatures, appointed to a special place or function, anointed and set apart for God's divine purpose. Satan (Lucifer) wanted to be like God.

When God anoints for His service, it is always for the glory of God. The anointing is not for us to promote ourselves. We are not anointed to boast on self, nor seek the glory, nor the praise and applause of men. Remain humble and never allow the applause of men to take you to a place where only the promotion of God can keep you. When the hand of God is upon the life of an individual that person will be effective and they will do what the occasion demands. When the LORD is using a person, whether that person realizes it or not, they are always in danger of having what I call a "Nebuchadnezzar moment".

Nebuchadnezzar was king of the Babylonian Empire, who reigned from 605 B.C.-562 B.C. He conquered nations, built an empire and enjoyed the fruits of his labor. He was a man lifted up in pride and would not give God his due glory. On a certain day, as he walked around his beautiful palace, admiring the splendor of his kingdom; he made a very prideful statement.

The king spake, and said, is not this great Babylon, that I have built for the house of the kingdom by the might of my power, and for the honour of my majesty?

Daniel 4:30

As he was speaking these very prideful and exalted words and boasting over his achievements, God took his kingdom away from him. Nebuchadnezzar lost his mind and for seven years he roamed about in the fields like a beast. He experienced a fall. He walked through the door of Proverbs 16:18, which warns us that pride goes before destruction and a haughty spirit before a fall. God used Babylon as his chastening rod for Israel. Nebuchadnezzar was employed by the sovereignty of God and in the end he realized that his greatness was not by his own strength! At the end of seven long years, Nebuchadnezzar lifted his eyes to heaven and his understanding returned to him. He praised, extolled and honored the Holy One of Israel, "blessed be he." Nebuchadnezzar in humility made this very powerful declaration about God: **"And those that walk in pride He is able to abase."**

As we caution ourselves against having a "Nebuchadnezzar moment," we should take a lesson from his life and remember when God begins to use us for His glory, no matter how anointed we think we are; no one should get the glory, but God. Humble is the way, as your understanding is enlightened by the Holy Spirit to know that it is an honor for the LORD to use you as He promotes you in His anointing to do the works of Jesus.

As I continued to look at the life of Nebuchadnezzar, I took a break and went for a walk; needing to catch up on some much needed exercise. Continuing to walk, I began to think on the subject of pride and examine myself to see how the enemy of my soul could have me walking in pride and I not realize it. Wow! What a revelation I received; that when it comes to the spirit of pride; one can't thoroughly examine one's self, because pride can hide and masquerade in many ways. It takes the work of the Holy Spirit to convict, find it hiding in dark places of the soul, root it out and help us get delivered from such a destructive force as pride. As I was walking, it was during the month of November when the leaves on the trees began to turn colors. As the season of fall rolled in, I took notice of the trees and the beautiful colors the leaves were experiencing. The colors ranged from green, yellow, orange, burnt orange and pomegranate red. Looking at the trees I thought; wow how beautiful. The second thought I had was, wow in a few more weeks the beauty of the leaves would have turned brown, fallen to the ground, and the limbs would be bare and seemingly barren. Still thinking about pride;

the colors of the leaves reminded me of a peacock. I smiled and mumbled under my breath, "**prideful as a peacock**." The changing of the leaves in the fall is beautiful and although the trees were not a symbol of pride, the Spirit of the Lord gave me this analogy. When the beauty of God's glory and anointing is upon an individual's life, they are like the beauty of the leaves changing on a tree. Meaning the anointing is attractive: it draws people and people will come with many applauds and accolades. People will say, man you sure can preach and wow you can sing. They will say things like, man of God, you sure can pray and my God, you can teach the Word! People will even have a tendency to compare you with well known preachers, teachers, evangelists, and singers, etc. and tell you that you are the next great so-in-so. If you continue to listen to the accolades and applauses of the people; pride will creep in. If you don't give God the glory, you'll lose your leaves (the anointing). The flow of Heaven's Oil will dry up and like the trees you will become bare (no anointing) and you'll be ineffective.

It's alright that people will encourage and even applaud you, just stay focused and don't become a causality of pride. Carriers of God's anointing should never want to attract attention to themselves, but should always point to Christ, "The Anointed One." If God has anointed you for His service and you are doing great exploits, never cater to and worship your own prestige. In doing so, you are in danger of becoming useless like a rotting loincloth (Jeremiah 13:1-10), which was a lesson about the way the Lord would let the pride of Judah and Jerusalem rot. Never heed the applause of the people, let "to God be the glory" be your anthem and mean it. Remember pride can be sneaky and you have to keep it in check. For example, who takes the mike on any given Sunday, without in some respect; a desire to display him or herself? Again pride is slick; for what minister of the gospel preaches, who never has any desire to display his gifts, talents and learning? Pride is sneaky, for who sings on any given Sunday without the appetite of a sign of admiration? Pride would love to make a fool out of all of us, and no one is exempt! Because pride can be so subtle in its manifestation; we all need to be on guard against it. We all need to be encouraged, but never get too caught up in the applause of people. The Lord will let you know if He's pleased with you. Why be puffed in any thing you do for the Lord when His word says that every man at his best state is but a vapor? Whatever we do in the name of Jesus, let it be in partnership with the Holy Spirit and we will be like a coffee maker making coffee, doing exactly what we are designed to do for the glory of the Father. Always remember to sidestep the praise of men, because the praise you get could very well belong to the Holy One of Israel, blessed be he.

I'm reminded of the life of Jose Cubero, a brilliant matador, who at the age of 21 was on the verge of a promising career. He injured a bull so seriously that it collapsed. Cubero considered the match with the bull was over as he thrust the sword in one final time. But the bull was not dead. So as he turned to acknowledge the applause of the crowd, the bull arose and lunged at the young matador. A horn pierced through his back puncturing his heart and he died. By no means am I saying this young man was a prideful person, but this tragic incident is a good example of getting caught up in the applause of people and losing focus.

As we guard against pride, we should pray that the Church as a whole will be on guard against the rising smoke of pride from the bottomless pit that would love to fill the atmosphere of any church. Pride is one of the most destructive forces that can plague an individual and the Church as a whole. It can eat away at a church like cancer if not put in check. To some degree, it's in every church and in every denomination. Pride will rear "its ugly head" and have certain churches not wanting to fellowship with smaller unknown or not so popular churches. It will manifest itself in division and condemnation of others who do not believe as they do. It always amazes me; yet it shouldn't, that there are denominations that believe that if you are not a part of their denomination, you will not go to heaven when you die. Is that not pride? I personally witnessed a man tell an older woman who was a born again believer in Jesus Christ that he was sorry, because if she died; she would not go to heaven. Why? She was not a part of his denomination. What staggered me was the fact that he said it with such conviction and confidence. When did a certain denomination become the single or true expression of the Church? WOW! It is stinkin' pride for any denomination to believe that God is the God of their denomination and theirs alone. Wow, when were we ever saved by denomination? Selah.

In the body of Christ, pride can become like a plague and its effects can be devastating to a ministry. Wherever you find the spirit of pride dominating a church, you will by and large find Heaven's Oil (the anointing) lacking. Without the anointing, a ministry will soon lose its spiritual vitality and power which will breed disunity. If disunity is allowed to breed it will birth contention, arguments, strife, debates, conflict and controversy. All the aforementioned are enemies to the flow of the anointing. Let's look at what David, the sweet Psalmist of Israel, says about unity and the anointing.

> *Behold, how good and how pleasant it is for brethren to dwell together in unity! It is like the precious ointment upon the head, that ran down upon the beard, even Aaron's beard: that went down to the skirts of his garments.*
>
> *Psalm 133:1-2*

David understood the blessedness of unity among the brethren. From a historical and prophetic viewpoint, this verse is better understood as a hope for reuniting the Northern and Southern Kingdoms of Israel (see Ezekiel 37:15-28), and from a broader sense it is often taken to refer to unity among the brethren or brotherly harmony. Unity is good and it is pleasant. When brethren dwell together in unity, it is a communion worthy to behold. Stop and behold your own family. I know that all families have their own set of issues and if you can't behold the unity in your own family, don't feel bad. But have you ever witnessed or fellowshipped with a family that seems as though they all loved each other? They were supportive and there was no hidden jealousy or strife in the clan. If you have ever witnessed that, wasn't it a communion to behold. David did say behold (look, gaze upon) the good and the pleasantness of unity. What about the unity among the family of Christ? When you find the saints on one accord, isn't that a sight to behold? The Spirit of God can move unhindered among a church that's unified! I say that because the Spirit of God is gentle like a dove and can be quenched if the atmosphere of a church is charged with disunity, strife, contention and the like. The fruit of the Spirit is the proof of unity and brotherly love, for when we come together for prayer, praise and worship; we want to be a sweet aroma unto the Lord, not a stench, nor a sounding brass or a tingling cymbal (see 1 Corinthians 13:1).

Much prayer is needed for our church leaders when promoted to certain positions because the temptations of pride is always lurking when a person is promoted to positions of power. Even the experience of a certain level of success in ministry will cause pride to rear its ugly head. Don't kid yourself, and think it not strange the temptation of pride, to try and plague a person in a position of power. It's dangerous to associate yourself with a position. Why? Because there's the danger that overtime a person will begin to think that they are more important and better than others and pride will cause a person to justify incorrect behavior towards others. Remember, we are anointed to serve, and to serve in the spirit of love. It's true, man can promote you to various positions, but only God can promote you in the anointing. If a person is in a position of leadership and they become cloaked in a spirit of pride, sooner or later the anointing upon their life will lift. They'll have positions, but no anointing -- exalted in their own mind, but no power. And let's not deceive ourselves into thinking that every individual who is promoted that his or her elevation and authority is from God. When man's agenda is more important than God's agenda, people will be promoted for various reasons. For example, the family member that is given a position in the body of Christ; instead of the person God has anointed for that particular position. And this is certainly not always the case, but what about the biggest givers money wise; will they be promoted based upon their ability to give? Let's be on guard against self-exaltation; for God will exalt the humble at the appointed time.

Whether it's an apostle, prophet, evangelist, pastor or teacher, people will treat you as though you are important and with respect because of your position, but don't be foolish and "wear pride like a necklace" (Psalm 73:6 NKJV). Once we know Christ personally and grow in Him, we will not have to worry about titles and positions to feel important, for He makes us whole and that alone makes us important. If you desire for Heaven's Oil to flow unhindered in your life, keep your vessel humble, wearing humility like the garb of a servant. In your intimate time with the Lord, tell Him you want a servant's heart like Christ. And when He begins to reveal any form of pride in you, though it may be painful, allow it to be liberating so that you can walk in your *'Divine Mission'* in the earth.

- Every one that is proud in heart is an abomination to the Lord and He will punish them (Proverbs 16:5)
- God hates pride and arrogance (Proverbs 8:13, 6:16-17)
- It is sin to have a high look and a proud heart (Proverbs. 21:4)
- For the day of the Lord of hosts shall be upon every one that is proud and lofty, and upon everyone that is lifted up; and he shall be brought low (Isaiah 2:12)

No man will ever be as humble as Jesus, but at least try and have the testimony of the humility of John the

Baptist -- HE **MUST INCREASE, BUT I MUST DECREASE** (John 3:30).

Chapter Four

Cold Love

One of the most powerful forces in the world is love. Love is crucial in operating in the anointing of God therefore carriers of His anointing must be committed to love. It was during the Feast of Passover, the last feast that Jesus would have with His disciples before His crucifixion when He instructed them on the subject of love. He said, "A new commandment I give unto you, that ye love one another as I have loved you, that ye also love one another. By this shall all men know that ye are my disciples, if ye have love one to another" (John 13:33-34). Sometimes the world may believe that individuals are a Christian or disciple of Christ by how they talk;

because people can be full of "religious jargon." Some people can perfect the art of sounding like a good Christian. The world may even believe that a person is a Christian just because they attend church. However, Jesus said the way that all (the world and the body of Christ) will know we are His (talmidim) disciples is by how we love one another. Yet, cold love seems to dominate or govern the lives of many believers and seemingly without any shame or conviction.

Christians would do well to take inventory of their heart to be sure they are not guilty of cold love. Your love walk is an area that the devil will aggressively try you in. Isn't it amazing how we say we love God and that Jesus is our Lord and Savior, but we don't love His people?

If a man say I love God and hateth his brother he is a liar; for he that loveth not his brother whom he hath seen, how can he love God whom he hath not seen?
1 John 4:20

The Word of God commands that His children love one another. While it is commanded that we walk in love, we have to make a quality decision to do so. There will be situations that will arise that will call for you to demonstrate the love of Jesus that's in you, but will you be able to deliver? Can I get a witness; walking in love is not always easy because the "old nature" wants to rise up in us when we have been badly treated? The ability to love people from the lovable to those that are very difficult can be done by the help of the Holy Spirit. We must ask for the Lord's help in those difficult cases, because as Christians, we are called to love. If you desire for the anointing of God to flow freely and without hindrance in your life, you must walk in faith, love and much patience.

The Lord Jesus is our ultimate and faultless example of how to teach, witness, pray, love, etc. He is our Christ, "the Anointed One," who went about doing good because of His love and compassion for people. God anointed Jesus of Nazareth with the Holy Ghost and with power, who went about doing good, and healing all that were oppressed of the devil for God was with him (Acts 10:38). God anointed Jesus and He will anoint you for His service to do good; but you have to walk in love and have no respect of person. Jesus touched the lives of all who were oppressed. As believers, can we do good to the down trodden, the broken, and those who the devil has exploited? Can we do good to the lepers-- those who the world consider unclean and incurable? Always take into consideration the anointing of God will flow from your life to the life of another if your love walk is unadulterated. In order for your love to be uncontaminated, know that you can't mix love with hatred, envy, strife, bitterness, pride and the like, it's just not pleasing to God. We brag about being anointed, but do we walk in love? We even boast about protecting our anointing, but do we walk in love? Do we aggressively protect our hearts against cold love? Are we any good by remaining sterile Christians by not wanting to deal with the unclean of the world? Is our love for our neighbor any different than the priest and the Levite in the parable of the "Good Samaritan" (Luke 10:25-37)?

In this parable Jesus exposes cold love and even hypocrisy. The priest and the Levites served in the Temple. They were divided into 24 courses. Remember

Luke tells us that Zechariah was of the eighth course of Abijah. Twice a year each division or course had a week on duty and because there were only 51 weeks in a year on a Jewish calendar; three weeks they all served. For a total of five weeks out of a year they served. What an honor it must have been to be a servant in the courts of the Lord and keep in mind a priest might go a lifetime and not be chosen for certain duties. Therefore, you did not want to do anything that would cause ritual uncleanness, as in touching a dead corpse. In Jewish culture, contact with a dead body was considered defilement of a person. In the parable of the "Good Samaritan," Jesus used the operative word "down" relating to the direction in which the priest and the Levite were traveling. After robbers had left a man half dead, a priest was traveling "down" the road and saw him. Likewise a Levite passed by, suggesting that he also was traveling "down". Jesus in telling this parable, made sure the listener understood the priest and the Levite were going "down" from Jerusalem. Jerusalem is about 3,000 feet above sea level to Jericho. Jericho is about 1,000 feet below sea level. Do you get the picture; the men were traveling "down"? If the priest and the Levite were leaving Jerusalem after their week of Temple duty, going down they had no excuse in not stopping to help the man that was beaten and left half dead on the side of the road. They had already served in the Temple, so helping the man would have not at this point affected their work. Had Jesus said the priest and the Levite were traveling "up" to Jerusalem, maybe the hearers would have made excuse for them in that touching what might have been a corpse, they could have incurred seven days of ritual impurity.

Cold love does not make room for loving thy neighbor as thy self. On the other hand, cold love will make room for a person to put their own affairs above someone else's need. An enemy, a Samaritan, a people who had a history of terrible hostility against the Jews, whom no one expected to help, put them to shame. It's sad but true, not all brotherly love or kindness will come from Christians or even "religious folk," but you can always count on it to come from the people who have the heartbeat of Jesus. The priest and the Levite had just left the Temple serving God, but didn't have time or the love to help a neighbor in need. They left God at the Temple. Isn't that like some Christians, they leave

Jesus at the church? People are hurting in the body of Christ and also in the world. So many people have been injured by Satan and left on the side of the road of "Life," wounded physically and emotionally and left to die. The Jesus in us should want to do something about it. We are not assigned to every need, but when it is in our ability to do something, let's not turn a cold heart towards the situation.

Jesus, a man of compassion, loved people period. If we walk in love, there can no longer be an "us" and "them" attitude. If its hunger, sickness, disease, prison bars, drugs, nakedness, motherless, fatherless, orphans or whatever the oppression may be, God has anointed us and given us power like Jesus to do good. We will have to answer to Him if we shut up our bowels of compassion and pass by on the other side of the road like the priest and the Levite, *in order to remain good clean sterile Christians*. When you are presented with the opportunity to help someone, do it and please give the glory to God and never overestimate the worth of your own contribution.

God, by the grace of the Holy Spirit has anointed the body of Christ to go forth in this earth realm and duplicate the works of Jesus. In order for the power of God and the anointing to flow, we must have faith and be obedient to His Holy Word. Jesus told His disciples, "If you love me keep my commandments". Our love for Jesus and the keeping of His commandments will guard against the demonic force of cold love. Cold love will cause the anointing to stagnate and when that happens, how can yokes be destroyed and burdens be removed? Out of the bowels of cold love, you will find strife, jealousy, discrimination, unforgiveness, bitterness, hatred, competition and the list goes on.

    Jesus, from the Mount of Olives, warned us that at the end of this age, because iniquity shall abound, the love of many shall wax cold (Matthew 24:12). The love of many will wax cold and those who once loved God will leave their first love like the church at Ephesus (Revelation 2:4). Many will openly desert love and some will corrupt love. So think it not strange when you have an encounter with cold love, even when it has manifested in the life of a believer and you're the recipient of that cold love. Your position is to do the will of the Father and that is to simply walk in love. We have to ask for the grace of the Holy Spirit to help us walk in love when offenses abound. It is important to realize that your walk with the Lord is only as real as your love walk. Hypocrisy can easily boast about a love for Jesus and not demonstrate that love to others. A believer whose life is governed by the Word of God, governed by an intimate relationship with the Lord, and governed by grace will be serious in their love for the brethren. If the Word governs us, we will love. If we have a relationship with the Lord, He will remind us to walk in love and mercy; which gives us the ability to see others as Jesus sees them and simply love. For some, the love walk may be easy and for some it may be difficult to love the unlovable for lack of a better term. With that said, we have to remember at one time or another, perhaps in the eyes of someone, maybe we were counted among the unlovable or difficult.

Brotherly love has come under tremendous attack. Satan has waged an all out attack on relationships at home and in the Church. The enemy of our soul knows all too well that a home or church divided against itself cannot stand. We can no longer believe the famous quote: We have met the enemy and he is us. That quote is what the devil wants us to believe that we are each others' enemy. Christians at times are so busy fighting each other that they have very little time or power left to battle the true enemies; principalities, powers and rulers of darkness and spiritual wickedness in high places. It is an awful and unpleasant thing to see "family warfare" within the Church. It is an alarming thing to see division, resentment, pride, competition, murdering tongues and all other evil works in the body of Christ due to cold love. Our Lord and Savior will not speak well of a church where the hearts of the people have grown cold towards Him and the people of God. The power and anointing of God will not flow in an atmosphere charged with cold love. You will have in that kind of church; perhaps, a piano, people in the pews, a choir, ushers and the preacher, but the Lord will be missing. If Satan has his way, he plays the cold love card and then stands back and watches disunity spread like a cancer. When it does, it spreads and creates spiteful cell groups or cliques in the body of Christ rapidly. This group will be against that group. The devil will have certain deacons fighting the preacher on every hand. He will have the preacher playing favoritism to the biggest givers in the church. He will make sure that there is at least one mean spirited usher on the door. The enemy will use whoever will yield to his promptings to create an atmosphere of cold love.

Cold love is a demonic stronghold that will not allow for unity; therefore, where there's disunity, again the power and the anointing of God will not operate. And so, we see strife and discord as the devil's means to keep the status of certain churches as weak and divided. This will eventually destroy that church's testimony or witness and when that happens, that church will lose its effectiveness in reaching the lost for Christ. Satan knows that a unified body of believers is a threat to his kingdom of darkness, so by whatever means necessary, and if the means is cold love, that is what he will use to put out that church's candlestick (light).

We have to realize the dangers of the demonic stronghold of cold love. We have to see it for what it is and how extremely unhealthy it is for the body of Christ. Cold love is a spiritual disease and when it is manifested, we make ourselves less available;

therefore, we discriminate and show respect of person. It will cause disloyalty and hatred for the brethren. It will shut down the power of prayer and again cripple the flow of the anointing for healing and deliverance to come forth. Cold love also allows for satanic ideas and doctrines to slither into the Church. Satan's design or idea for some churches is to keep them operating in cold love; keeping them unconverted and unspiritual and in doing so, carnality will have dominion. If carnality has dominion, the people will remain in bondage to self (flesh), babes in Christ, cold-hearted, un-anointed and unable to engage in spiritual warfare victoriously.

It is also a scheme of the devil to get us to think that as Christians, we can still please the Lord even though we don't walk in love. Jesus told His disciples, if your brother has anything against you, to go and be reconciled with thy brother before you come to the altar to offer up thy gift to Him (see Matthew 5:23-24.) We are to walk in love; we are not even supposed to wait until the offended brother comes to us. We are to seek them out and be reconciled. In doing so, our worship and what we bring to God's altar will be acceptable. The external act in worship may look good on the outside, but Jesus is concerned with the matters of the heart. He that comes to worship his Creator **filled** with spite, hatred, envy, malice and at war with his brethren, is a counterfeit worshipper. God is not deceived, and neither will He be mocked with phony worship. Can I get a witness? Have you ever been in your devotion time, and gone away empty because you have not done what is right towards others? Could it be that your worship and devotion was not at all pleasing unto the Lord because of some sort of unresolved issue (ought) with a brother or sister?

There is even the tendency to make into an idol what others have done to us and we cherish and hold onto improper feelings towards others in our heart. If that is the case, God will not throw you away and neither will He condemn you. However, because He loves you, He will convict you in love and our Helper the Holy Spirit will assist you in your love walk as you yield and give your heartaches and pain to Him.

At this point you can stop reading this book and without any condemnation, be reconciled with a brother or sister and remain in right standing with God, for His love, grace and mercy will see you through. In doing so, you will experience a freedom to worship your Maker in spirit and in truth. The power and the anointing of God will flow unhindered in your life when your love walk is in line with the Word of God. Because you love without compromise, God will be able to use you in His service and manifest His power and anointing in miraculous ways.

A lawyer, an expert in the Mosaic Law, asked Jesus of the commandments, which is the greatest? Jesus said unto him, "You shall love the Lord your God with all your heart, with all your soul, and with all your mind. This is the first and great commandment. The second is like it, you shall love your neighbor as yourself" (Matthew 22:37-39 NKJV). This passage of scripture is the answer to cold love. As you love God and desire His presence, the Lord will pour into your heart a greater love for Him and a love for thy neighbor, which will eradicate cold love. As I think about loving your neighbor as yourself, I'm reminded of a story told by Thomas Lindberg of two neighbors who were rivals. Two shopkeepers were bitter rivals and their stores were directly across the street from each other. They would spend each day keeping track of each others' business. If one got a customer, he would glance across the street and smile in triumph at his rival. One night an angel appeared to one of the shopkeepers in a dream and said, "I will give you anything you ask, but whatever you receive, your competitor will receive twice as much." Would you be rich? You can be very rich, but he will be twice as wealthy. Do you wish to live a long and healthy life? You can, but his life will be longer and healthier. What is your desire? The man frowned, thought for a moment, and then said, "Here is my request: Strike me blind in one eye!" Wow! If the one shopkeeper was struck blind in one eye that meant his neighbor would be blind in both eyes. Talk about love for thy neighbor! Is that cold love or what? To love thy neighbor as thyself is to do unto others as you would have them do unto you. It is not to impose onto others what you would not want done to you. When someone responds to you with cold love, as a Christian, you are to respond back with the energy of love. Respond with agape love, a love that is completely selfless that will pull down the stronghold of cold love. I truly understand that love is warfare because there will be times when you won't feel like operating in love, but again our Helper the Holy Spirit, the Spirit of Wisdom will see you through.

Never justify incorrect behavior towards others even if they have wronged you. Yes it may be hard not to react but bear in mind others are watching to witness how you respond. Jesus said that by the love we have for one another, all men shall know that we are His disciples. Again, it's not by our church attendance, dress or manner of speech, nor is it by the pride of rank and wealth, but it is the love we have for one another that is the vital evidence that we are followers of Jesus Christ, and people will see and know it. If we are followers of Christ and we fail to walk in love, then we show cause to suspect our sincerity. As carriers of God's anointing, we must guard against the demonic force of cold love. We are co-laborers with Christ and He wants to work through us to touch the lives of people that are bound by the unfruitful works of darkness. Believers cannot do the works of Jesus if we are bound by the force of cold love. There is a harvest of souls waiting for laborers to minister the love of Christ to them. Church can no longer be about meeting our needs; but about a divine mission to meet the needs of others. Forget what everyone else is doing or not doing; ask the Lord to give you a servant's heart; a heart full of compassion to love and go forth into the harvest of souls and minister.

When Jesus was sending the seventy out to spread the gospel, He said, "the harvest was plentiful, but the laborers were few and that we are to pray that the Lord of the harvest would send forth laborers." The harvest is an ever-present reality, there's always a soul out there that need Jesus' saving grace. If you leave a harvest in the field to long it will ultimately spoil. For example, a farmer will tell you that when a watermelon has ripened, you have to get the melon off the vine and off the ground or in time, it will spoil. How many souls have been left un-harvested, leaving them in the field (the world) for the devil to spoil the soul of man with unfruitful works of darkness? How do you view the harvest in your community? Do you judge sinners without compassion? Do you look at the harvest through the eyes of compassion or the eyes of cold love? Have you received the grace of God in vain? Prayerfully, your answer is absolutely not. Then guard against cold love and pray that the Lord of the harvest will qualify and commission you for His work. Remember to operate in love, and know that one word from Jesus can turn resistance to surrender, and doubt to fervent faith! Go forth and love thy neighbor!

- If thy neighbor speaks peace to you and the Holy Spirit has shown you the malice in their heart towards you, love them still.
- If thy neighbor thinks differently than you, love them straight on.
- If thy neighbor has a bigger home, fancier car, clothes, (etc., love them the more.
- If thy neighbor is of a different religion or denomination, we still must show love.
- If thy neighbor is a heathen, love them still.
- If thy neighbor has spoken ill of you, love them still.
- If thy neighbor rejoices in your adversity, love them the more.

- If thy neighbor dislikes you and has issues with you because of **BORROWED OFFENSE,** love them the more. When a person has borrowed the offense of others, they will dislike you based upon someone else's offense towards you. Take heed, when your friend is offended; support them; but beware of taking up their offense against the offender. When offense happens, ask God for the grace to bear it.
- If thy neighbor (fill in the blank), you must love them still.

It is easy to say to a brother or sister, I love you and decorate and embellish it with religious lace; but God will see right through hypocritical, insincere and phony love. WOW! Let's not be counted among those whose love will wax cold before the return of the Lord.

Chapter Five

Grieving the Holy Spirit

And grieve not the Holy Spirit of God, whereby ye are sealed unto the day of redemption.

Ephesians 4:30

No one will be able to receive a greater measure of the anointing if they live a lifestyle that grieves the Holy Spirit of God. Grief is a keen mental suffering or distress over affliction or loss. Simply put, it is mental distress. As carriers of the anointing, believers must be sensitive to the Holy Spirit; otherwise, we can find ourselves experiencing things brought about by our failure to pay attention to and yield to the Spirit of the Living God. If we're aware and receptive to the Spirit, then our steps will be guided by the Lord. The Spirit of God is dwelling within believers, and we don't ever want to cause bitter feelings towards our guest that abides with us. I believe to become sensitive to the Holy Spirit; we must have communion or fellowship with Him daily. Be so ever cautious of the devil; that will come with so many distractions daily, in order to keep a believer out of intimate fellowship with the Spirit of the Living God. We must violently turn our will over to the Lord and ask for the grace to do it. I used the word violently because the enemy fights believers in the area of their will. We can't be anointed and walk in the power of God if we ignore the Spirit of God. The enemy knows that if we continue to do things "our way," instead of "God's way;" it can lead to a barren, fruitless, and unproductive end. Obeying the voice of the Holy Spirit will always lead to life. The Holy Spirit speaks expressly; meaning in a very definite way. When your ear has been trained to hear His voice, and in obedience to Him, you do whatever has been spoken; the Person of the Holy Spirit is pleased and not grieved. Hear me beloved, the anointing flows through an obedient vessel. When the Holy Spirit is talking to you and governing your life; the enemy of your soul will always rear its ugly head to try and sway you to go in another direction. The Holy Spirit will give you the grace you need to override the voice of rebellion and do that which is pleasing in His sight.

The anointing of God will flow unhindered in the life of the believer who has reverence for the Holy Spirit. The Holy Spirit is not an "it," but a Person worthy to receive our surrender. It is a good thing to remember to treat the Holy Spirit not as an experience or merely a power or influence, but as a Person. He is a divine Person of infinite power, glory, holiness, majesty and wisdom. He has come into a believer's heart to make His abode there and take ownership of their lives and to make use of our lives for the glory of God.

As Christians, we are never alone. Jesus gave us the Holy Spirit as a Comforter, ever present with us; therefore, how we treat the Spirit of God is most important. We must learn to trust the Spirit in helping us in our walk of faith. We must develop a confidence in His love and come to a place wherein we realize that

He longs to bless us and help us with our weaknesses. He is our gift and we should appreciate the gift the Lord has given us with love and honor. Anointed men and women of God will express to you how they have made the Holy Spirit their friend. They speak of how they honor the role He plays in their daily lives. The Holy Spirit is to be treated in a way that speaks of love, honor and appreciation. When you honor the relationship and fellowship that you have with the Holy Spirit, He will infuse you with His power, causing the anointing to flow at liberty in your life. With the help of the Holy Spirit, you will be able to live a victorious and conquering life.

There's a passage of scripture in the Bible in which one characteristic of the personality of the Holy Spirit comes across as tender and gentle.

And grieve not the Spirit of God, whereby ye are sealed unto the day of redemption.
Ephesians 4:30

The Spirit of the Living God by no means is distant, aloof or impersonal. He is a holy Person who comes to dwell in the hearts of born again believers. He's one who clearly sees every deed we perform, every word we speak and every thought we entertain. If there is anything in word, deed or thought that is ungodly or unholy, the Holy Spirit could possibly be grieved by it. The words we speak; let them be in agreement with the Word of God. The deeds we do; let them be edifying. The thoughts we have; let them be godly, thinking on things that are honest, just and things that are of a good report. Let us cast down wicked imaginations. How often a Christian will say something, do something or go places that they wouldn't want the pastor to know about? Some Christians have mastered the art of hiding sin; therefore, they think they are covered. There's One more holier than the pastor, that we should respect, lead a holy life and walk softly in His presence. He's an ever-present Person that sees all and He cannot bear or endure sin.

    Christians can't be effective if they ignore or grieve the Holy Spirit. Not only will a person be unable, they will be fully unable to do the will of the Lord without the help of the Holy Spirit. The people of God can and sometimes do grieve the Holy Spirit. When this happens, we have to repent with godly sorrow and move on. There are many ways to grieve the Holy Spirit, and here are just a few.

- Chasing after the temptations that are in the world through lust
- Entertaining filthy, wicked and iniquitous imaginations
- Open sin that brings disgrace upon the body of Christ
- Neglecting prayer
- Treating the Holy Spirit as if He is an experience and not a divine Person
- Neglecting the Word of God
- No gratitude or appreciation to Jesus for all He has done for you and yet wanting more (greed)
- A Christian, but no reverential fear of God
- Cold love among the saints and being hostile to the law of love (Christians mistreating Christians)
- Stubbornness against the Will of God and resisting "Truth" (God's Holy Word))
- Resisting sanctification

- Indulging in appetites and passions that ruin your spirituality and your witness before mankind

This list could go on and on because there are many ways the Holy Spirit can be grieved, but to keep it simple, sin grieves Him. As you examine the above list or the things you have going on in your own life, if you are guilty of bringing grief to the Spirit of the Living God repent and make it right. I personally know of ways I have caused my friend (Holy Spirit) grief and without any condemnation, He gave me the opportunity to repent and make proper some things. It is a daily walk or communion with the Spirit to become sensitive to Him, so that our actions are not unpleasant, distasteful or offensive in His sight. When I think of how often I have let the devil in, I'm so grateful that the Holy Spirit didn't withdraw from me. There have been times when I felt as though He withdrew my sense of His presence in order to get my attention. I want you to know that during those times my soul felt dry and parched. I've learned to appreciate and value Him more and more. The fact that the Spirit of the Living God keeps me and helps me persevere daily is a multitude of miracles, grace, mercy and love. He is faithful in helping me face trials, struggles, misunderstandings and temptations. He is there to celebrate with me in the victories of life. I'm learning to develop a greater or deeper friendship with the Holy Spirit. My spiritual growth and the ability to flow in the power and anointing of God and to do His will depends upon the Holy Spirit, faith, grace and my obedience. He is available to help all to walk in their divine purpose. He's there to help you become aligned with the mind of Christ and the will of God for your life, which brings empowerment and dominion in the life of a believer.

An individual who has grieved the Holy Spirit habitually could find some or all of the following signs manifesting in their lives.

- Your Christian walk is sub-standard and anemic, weak or feeble
- You will feel the loss of His presence
- Instead of a watered garden, a dry, parched and thirsty soul

- Your "hallelujah" shout is nothing more than a sounding brass and a tinkling cymbal
- Your ministry or life will yield no fruit and if it does, it will be fruit that will not remain.
- Doubt and unbelief will plague the mind
- Loss of Christian joy
- Don't feel close to God
- Struggle to have peace in times of trouble
- The mind will see truth very dimly
- No interest in reading and studying the Bible: It has become a boring and dead letter.

If any of these have manifested in your life because you have habitually grieved the Holy Spirit, acknowledge and repent of any disobedience or rebellion in your life. Keep in mind, the devil will always be at hand to condemn you even after you have repented and asked for forgiveness. The Holy Spirit will convict; but not condemn you and He will give you the grace to walk in your forgiveness. Isn't it wonderful, that although a Person, the Holy Spirit is not like human beings that will hold a grudge for a lifetime? When we repent with godly sorrow for any grief that we have caused Him, He is faithful and just to forgive us. He will wipe the slate clean so to speak and start afresh in your life, giving you the opportunity to make Him your very best Friend; thereby, enjoying a restored relationship with Him. Forgiveness is easy for Him. Unlike us, we can be mad and remain bitter for a long time because of grief others have caused in our lives. We can remain in a state of bitterness and unforgiveness over some of the most trivial things. Yes we can! How about being mad at grandma for years for giving your sister the biggest piece of Jelly cake? Now the enemy starts on them right early in life, grooming them and bathing their soul with rejection and resentment. We don't have to carry bitterness for years; the Holy Spirit is there to help us in the process of forgiveness. For some walking in forgiveness may come instantly and for others it could take a little time; but remember we do have a Helper.

In this hour of great deception, with the enemy of our soul relentlessly pursuing the people of God, we need the help of the Holy Spirit to be the "conqueror" and not the "conquered." We can't afford to live a life that grieves the Spirit of the Living God and be victorious. Christians have to be alert and sober and not allow the devil to deceive them into thinking that ignoring the Holy Spirit is a harmless act. We cannot live a life that is independent and absent from the jurisdiction of the Person of the Holy Spirit. There's nothing more dangerous and threatening to an individual than a spirit of self-rule or independence from the Spirit of God; because you will lack the wisdom of heaven and you will have to survive life by your own wits or understanding.

How many people can testify to making mistakes that have cost them dearly? For some, it has set them back some years, because they leaned to their own wits? King Solomon in his wisdom admonishes us to lean not unto our own understanding because he knew that there are many paths in life to travel. He tells us that if we attend to wisdom, by acknowledging God in all our ways, He would direct our paths in life as well as lead us not into temptation, but deliver us from the evil one; who desires to yoke you with the unfruitful works of darkness.

The Body of Christ has a Helper (Holy Spirit) who is there for us, to help us operate in the power and anointing of God so that we don't have to succumb to the yoke of the enemy. Yokes are destroyed because of the anointing (Isaiah 10:27). A yoke is a wooden beam placed on the neck of oxen or other animals to enable them to pull carts and plow fields. When the yoke is placed upon the neck of the oxen and bound, they become as slaves unable to move on their own. An animal bound to a yoke by this means, is enslaved. That's exactly what the enemy of our soul wants to do to us, enslave us. He wants sin to master us. Satan has an arsenal of devices to use as yokes. Yokes are synonymous with oppression, burdens, bondage, load, repression and annoyance. Satan has placed different yokes upon people and he has enslaved them. There's a harvest of souls waiting for an anointed vessel of God to minister deliverance not by might, nor by the power of man, but by the Spirit of the Living God. We are not to be ignorant of Satan's devices lest he gets an advantage over us (2 Corinthians 2:11). The enemy of our soul comes to steal, kill, and destroy. The devil knows that sin is an equal opportunity destroyer. He bids all who will come, to eat at his table of sin where darkness and death feeds the soul of those who are servants (slaves) of sin. We need the help of the Holy Spirit to discern the hand of the enemy and to triumph over the wiles and devices of the devil.

There was a period of time in the body of Christ when it seemed as though prosperity teaching was the way to go and maybe for some the only way. It seems as though I heard, "get yo' money and yo' honey, get yo' man and get yo' land, get yo' house and yo' spouse," I heard this preached so much until I went WOW, Christianity has come down to getting a bunch of stuff from God! I'm **not** at all against "prosperity teaching," matter of fact, I get excited and in expectation when I hear it. Yes! God wants us prosperous in every area of our lives, but when the enemy has attacked your family, you can't stick your Mercedes in the nostrils of Satan and say, "My Mercedes rebuke you Satan!" You want the power of the Holy Ghost backing you. Let's have some balance, there's nothing wrong with "stuff" and "things," but desire the anointing from on high that destroys the yoke of the enemy and the unfruitful works of darkness. Also in defense of the Holy Spirit, let not the body of Christ put so much emphasis on the "five-fold ministry" until we lay aside and over look the ministry of the Holy Spirit. Sometimes we want a title so bad we are willing to sidestep the ministry of the Holy Spirit to root out, cut asunder, cleanse us, and prepare us to walk in the office of an apostle, prophet, evangelist, pastor and/or teacher. This grieves the Holy Spirit because it is He that gives you supernatural enabling power to serve in the Kingdom of God and even in the marketplace and be effective. You cannot circumvent the ministry of the Holy Spirit and neither can you continue to grieve Him and expect heaven's oil (the anointing) to flow in your life. Let us be so ever grateful for the Spirit of the Living God, who dwells within us, to empower us to live the life of the conqueror and not the conquered.

    Today, if you hear His (Holy Spirit) voice, do not harden your heart. Today, if you have caused the Spirit grief, repent and come to a place in your heart where you honor Him, for He is our:

- Guide: He guides and protects us from error. He will guide you into all truth.
- Counselor: He is our "parakletos" called along side to help, counsel, advise and support.
- Sanctifier: He helps free us from things in our lives that are contrary to the nature of God.
- Helper: He helps us to live a life governed by the Word of God. He helps us to be in unity with the will of God.
- Convictor: He convicts believers of sin, wrong actions and attitudes contrary to the Word of God. He helps believers to be mindful of what the Word of God expects from them and to govern themselves accordingly.
- Teacher: He shows us how to take "Truth" the Word of God and wisely apply it to life. He is the Spirit of Wisdom that teaches us how to receive the Word of God in our hearts.
- Communicator: He will communicate the desires, plans, purpose and Will of God for your life. He will speak prophetically to you concerning your future and the plans that God has for your life.

The Holy Spirit is immeasurably greater than what I can express to you, but know that no one has more love and concern for developing you into the person that God has called you to be than the Holy Spirit. Make Him your very best friend and live life more abundantly. Develop an intimate relationship with Him and experience Heaven's Oil being poured upon your life.

Chapter Six

A Religious Spirit

Religious Spirit: It is a spirit that motivates and encourages faithfulness to religious practices in such a way as to oppose the works of Christ and protect the status quo.

The religious spirit can affect believers and they can be unaware of its workings in their lives. That's the nature of being deceived; you can become completely unaware of your condition. It is what we don't know that can ensnare us. Deception is a tool of Satan and we are warned that we are not to be ignorant of Satan's devices, lest he should get an advantage over us (2 Corinthians 2:11).

When we consider the anointing and the power of the Holy Spirit, believers can no longer afford to be ignorant of the nature of the religious spirit. Be not deceived beloved, no one is above being attacked by this spirit; so before we look at others, let us examine ourselves first. The personality or essence of the religious spirit is to substitute religious exercise and religious activity for the power of the Holy Spirit. Again, its major objective is for the Church to have a form of godliness, but deny the power thereof (2 Timothy 3:5). Our heavenly Father is not looking for external forms of godliness and neither is He moved by dead forms of religion. To keep it simple, God desires to have a relationship with His people. God gave man relationship and man gave God religion. From the beginning of time it's been all about relationship. God is concerned with the heart of man, not a bunch of religious activity that caters to the flesh or carnal mind. Remember, God's eyes are on those who are submitted to Him as well as those who pretend submission. Keep in mind the religious spirit is big on pretense.

Our lives are transformed into the image or character of Jesus by the grace of the Holy Spirit. On the other hand, the religious spirit drives people to think that they become righteous by self-effort and being disciplined; ignoring the work of the Holy Spirit. Thanks to Jesus Christ our Lord and Savior, we do not have to try to obtain righteousness through our own effort. The Holy Spirit will work a work in you so that the righteousness of the Lord becomes a part of your life. The religious spirit drives people to say the right thing and perform a certain way when people are looking. This spirit motivates a person to talk a good talk as to appear to be a "good" Christian; yet they lack the regenerating work of the Holy Spirit. No matter what good deeds a man does and no matter how many rituals, set of laws or traditions man keeps, he cannot make himself righteous. Man cannot justify (make righteous) himself. Any attempt at righteousness on our part, no matter how impressive, would without measure fall short of the holiness and righteousness of our Lord. So we give thanks to God that through His Son Jesus, we obtain righteousness. We must accept by faith what Jesus did for us and never trust in our own righteousness but simply grow in the grace of God.

Jesus shared a parable about two men who went to the Temple to pray; one a Pharisee and the other a publican (Luke 18:9-14). It was a parable about one man trusting in himself and his righteousness while despising another whose social-economic class was lower. The Pharisee stood and prayed, thanking God that he was not as other men. He told God that he was glad that he was not an extortionist, unjust, an adulterer or even as the publican that prayed. He went on to tell God about his own righteousness and good deeds. He bragged about his fasting and even how often he fasted. He even blew his own horn about his tithing from all he possessed. The publican, on the other hand, standing afar off, wouldn't lift up so much his eyes unto heaven, but smote upon his breast saying God be merciful to me a sinner. Jesus said this man went down to his house justified rather than the other. Jesus ended the parable with a warning, for everyone that exalts himself shall be abased, and he that humbles himself shall be exalted. The religious spirit deceives an individual into seeing themselves as superior to others. This Pharisee felt that he had earned his right standing with God and the publican had not, and for that reason he could sing his own praises. Thank God for His amazing grace, for grace destroys any man's right to boast about works. Be careful when you present to Jesus the "good stuff" you've done, He just might reply unto you, "Yes, but one thing thou lackest," and you might not like the instructions following (see Mark 10:17-21). The religious spirit doesn't make way for an individual to walk in the freedom and grace of God. When you trust in your own righteousness, you deny the power and the anointing of the Holy Spirit access into your heart to reveal to you areas in your life that need deliverance and healing. Self-righteousness is a yoke of the enemy; but no matter how tight the yoke is, it can be destroyed by the anointing of the Holy Spirit.

    The religious spirit welcomes empty worship and reverence that provides lip service unto a holy God; while the heart is distant or far from Him. It thrives on the status quo of having a form of godliness, denying the regenerating and sanctifying influence of the Holy Spirit to change a life into one that is pleasing to the Lord. This spirit attempts to take control of the Gospel to bring shallowness to the genuine message of Jesus. This spirit without any hindrance, loves for the Word of

God to be preached, but not lived. Remember, the devil does not care whether you go to hell through the church or through the world and he is right happy with the individual who attends church Sunday after Sunday; yet, remaining unconverted. Satan loves hypocrisy and he encourages playacting in the house of the Lord, giving him an open door to come in and participate in a church service, so that the people can leave declaring that they had church; yet, remaining destitute of the life of Christ. Selah! Religious folk can only stand as much of Jesus that will make them feel good about themselves while holding onto a "false-carnal security" in belonging to a local church. The religious spirit will encourage people to be lovers of pleasure more than lovers of God. It will have a person on edge in church, sitting in the pews having an *"I can't wait until the service is over attitude,"* because they love not the things of God. Keep in mind that all religious deceptions work to draw the people of God away from glorifying, worshipping and enjoying Jesus to a life of fulfilling what the flesh desires.

The anointing and the power of the Holy Ghost to regenerate, to sanctify and influence is offensive to the religious spirit. We see this in the life of Christ, the Anointed One, in His dealings and rebuke given to the Pharisees. The religious spirit opposes the anointing and power of the Holy Spirit to transform lives. It was a religious spirit or attitude that opposed Christ when He healed a man in the synagogue on the Sabbath (Luke 6:6-11). The Pharisees were very out-spoken in opposing the ministry of Jesus. The religious spirit is synonymous with the Pharisees, but before I go any further I want to say a few things about the Pharisees. Surprisingly, not all Pharisees were bad or hypocrites. To say so is like saying all Baptists, all Methodists, all Catholics, all Pentecostals, etc. are hypocrites. Jewish history tells us that there were seven classes of Pharisees (1) Shoulder Pharisee; (2) Wait-a-little Pharisee; (3) Blind Pharisee; (4) Pestle Pharisee; (5) Ever-reckoning Pharisee; (6) God-fearing Pharisee; and (7) God-loving Pharisee.

According to Jewish history, during the first century there were more than six thousand Pharisees who refused to take an oath of allegiance to Herod because of their belief that the Messiah and His age or reign was just on the horizon. The king punished them with a fine, which was paid by Pherora's wife who happened to be Herod's sister-in-law. We know that there were Pharisees that served God in genuine devotion and were followers of Jesus. Nicodemus who was a Pharisee was a follower of Jesus. Gamaliel, a Pharisee, doctor of the law and teacher of the Apostle Paul, argued for open-mindedness and patience from the Sanhedrin when Peter and the other disciples were brought before the council, saving the Lord's disciples (Acts 5:33-39). It was certain Pharisees that warned Jesus about Herod's intention to kill Him (Luke 13:31). So we see that not all Pharisees were hypocrites. Remember, if a religious group has its villainous characters, it also has its saints.

When the Lord Jesus expressed His disapproval for the hypocrisy of the Pharisees, He pronounced a "woe" over their lives. He rebuked them on many occasions for having what is called a religious spirit. I made the statement earlier that the religious spirit is synonymous with the Pharisees. This spirit will drive or motivate people to be seen of men, making the outer appearance the major concern and putting less emphasis on the attitude of the heart. The Pharisees were guilty of this. Jesus said that the individual who performs to be seen by men to appear religious, He likened that individual to whitewashed sepulchers (graves). He said you indeed appear beautiful on the outside, but are full of dead men's bones and of all uncleanness (Matthew 23:27). The nature of the religious spirit fights against a person yielding to the work of the Holy Spirit and the anointing of God to destroy those hidden yokes (sin) that causes a person to be full of iniquity inwardly; yet, appearing righteous unto men outwardly. This spirit does not want the inner man fixed up so to speak; yet, it doesn't mind if the outer is adorned with "religious fluff."

What a strong rebuke, when Jesus compared the Pharisees "religious folk" with whitewashed sepulchers. What a way to spur them to thinking and to look at themselves. You see, during the preparation time for Jewish festivals in Jerusalem, workmen would whitewash the tombs, making them appear pretty and clean on the outside. The whitewashing also served to identify a gravesite and a warning to the pilgrims traveling to the feast, not to touch or walk over a grave so that they would not bring upon themselves defilement. No one wanted to be declared ritually unclean while they journeyed to Jerusalem to participate in the Festivals. The graves were highly respected but they still carried the contagious taint of a dead body. The Pharisees, like the whitewashed sepulchers looked attractive, but were unclean inwardly as if filled with dead men's bones. What a rebuke and what a painted picture of the religious spirit, pretty on the outside; yet, warring against the anointing and power of the Holy Spirit to work on the inside to help a person make the necessary change(s) of the heart.

With the help of the Holy Ghost, it would be wise to take personal inventory of our lives to make sure we are not guilty of being influenced by a religious spirit because this spirit can goad you into the arena of pride. I admonish you in this because sometimes there can be the ingredient of pride even in your personal sacrifice. We may have given up some things to serve the Lord like the Pharisee in Luke 18:9-14). We may have prayed, fasted, served and given, but when we desire others to know we do these things; then our actions will be for the approval and admiration of men. Take heed you could be bowing thy neck to the yoke of a religious spirit. Here are some warning signs of the religious spirit:

- They honor God with counterfeit lips, while holding their heart far away from Him. This people honor Me with their lips, but their heart is far from Me (Mark 7:6).
- They make the external the main focus rather than focusing on matters of the heart. Woe to you scribes and Pharisees, hypocrites, for you make clean the outside of the cup and of the platter, but within they are full of extortion and excess (Matthew 23:25).
- Their worship is that of empty words denying their heart in having a relationship with God (see Mark 7:6-7). Anyone can praise God, but it takes a relationship with Him in order to worship in spirit and in truth.
- Whatever a person does for the Kingdom of God, they want to be seen

by men. But all their works they do for to be seen of men (Matthew 23:5a).

- They are very prideful of their spiritual maturity and will make a big deal over someone else's immaturity. When we see spiritual immaturity, we are to pray for that individual to continue to grow in grace and progress in the things of the Lord. We are all a work in progress.
- They have a heart that is dull, unreceptive and uninterested in the things of God. They are in church, but not in Christ.
- They are driven by the religious spirit to see the wrong in others while ignoring the plank that is in their own eye.
- They are enticed by the religious spirit to borrow someone else's tongues ("speaking in tongues") to sound religious. Wow! If they can sound like so-in-so, then they can sound real spiritual.

- They are more excited about church activity over having a relationship with Jesus.
- They believe themselves to be closer and more in tune with God and spiritual things than others.
- They pray with carnal motives, focusing on how they sound to the ears of the listeners. Praying to impress flesh.
- They are groomed by the religious spirit to appear pious externally, but inwardly corrupt.

To some degree, all of us are subject to the influence of a religious spirit. So before we begin to point it out in others, let's yield to the wisdom of the Holy Spirit to reveal to us if we have been seduced by this spirit. There is hope and there is help for anyone who has been influenced by the religious spirit. Your help lies in the anointing and power of the Holy Spirit to set the captive free. Ask the Holy Spirit to help you discern the nature of this spirit and thereby you will be able to resist and not give place to the devil. When we consider the body of Christ, we are in a very critical hour. And we must understand that we can no longer afford to waste any more time, talents, money or energy perfecting a "form of godliness." Selah!

About the Author:

Marilyn Reed is an ordained minister who has a deep appreciation for Heaven's Oil (the anointing) of God. She gives God the glory for choosing and anointing her to be a vessel to spread the Gospel of Jesus Christ. With a humble heart, she always tells the Lord: "What an honor to be a servant in the courts of the Lord!" Marilyn is a God chaser who loves the presence of the LORD, because in His presence is where she finds herself being equipped to handle the trials, temptations and storms of life. She understands that in His presence is where He will smear on the oil of the anointing that will enable her to help others overcome the unfruitful works of darkness. Her heart's desire is to see deliverance in the lives of God's people and the captive set free to know Jesus as their Lord and Savior. She realizes that the "Harvest of Souls" is always a present day reality, and she thanks God that she is a co-laborer with Christ to share with others that the Kingdom of Heaven is at hand. Marilyn is eternally thankful to Jesus Christ, who enables her, for that he counted me faithful, putting me into the ministry (1 Timothy 1:12).

Marilyn attended the University of Arkansas Monticello. She is the wife of U.S. Reed. She is the mother of two beautiful children, a son Alex and a daughter Toni. She is the proud grandmother of two, McKenzie and Adyson. But above all she is the product of "GRACE AND MERCY."

I WANT TO HEAR FROM YOU!

If this book has been an inspiration to you and has encouraged you in any kind of way, write or email me and share your story. Thanks for your feedback.

Contact the Author:

Marilyn Reed

P.O. Box 6422

Pine Bluff, Arkansas 71611

E-mail: maguy.reed@hotmail.com

Phone: 1-870-329-1053

www.ingramcontent.com/pod-product-compliance
Lightning Source LLC
Chambersburg PA
CBHW071138090426
42736CB00012B/2153